All About Dinosaurs

Velociraptor

Daniel Nunn

Heinemann LIBRARY
Chicago, Illinois

Edited by Daniel Nunn and James Benefield
Designed by Tim Bond
Picture research by Tracy Cummins
Production by Helen McCreath
Originated by Capstone Global Library Ltd
Printed in the United States of America in
North Mankato, Minnesota. 042015 008911RP

Library of Congress Cataloging-in-Publication Data
Nunn, Daniel, author.
  Velociraptor / Daniel Nunn.
    pages cm.—(All about dinosaurs)
  Summary: "This book takes a very simple look at the
Velociraptor dinosaur, examining what it looked like,
what it ate, how it behaved, and its special skills and
features such as its sharp teeth and claws. The book
also discusses how we know about Velociraptor today,
showing where fossils are found and how scientists put
them together."—Provided by publisher.
  Includes bibliographical references and index.
  ISBN 978-1-4846-0208-9 (hb)—ISBN 978-1-4846-0215-7
(pb) 1. Velociraptor—Juvenile literature. 2. Dinosaurs—
Juvenile literature. I. Title.

  QE862.S3N866 2015
  567.912—dc23   2013040469

Acknowledgments
We would like to thank the following for permission to
reproduce photographs: Alamy p. 21 (© Kayte Deioma/
ZUMAPRESS.com); Corbis pp. 17 (©Mark Stevenson /
Stocktrek Images), 18 (© Walter Geiersperger); Getty
Images pp. 4, 8, 15 (Daniel Eskridge/Stocktrek Images),
11 (Yuriy Priymak/Stocktrek Images), 19 (DANI POZO/
AFP), 23 (Ulrich Baumgarten); The Image Works p. 12
(©The Natural History Museum); Science Source pp. 6
(José Antonio Peñas), 20 (John Mitchell); Shutterstock
pp. 5a, 9, 10, 13 (Michael Rosskothen), 5b (iSIRIPONG),
5c (defpicture), 5d (Mogens Trolle), 7 left (Ralf Juergen
Kraft), 7 right (Chepko Danil Vitalevich), 10 background
(design36), 27 (tratong); Superstock pp. 16 (Kevin
Eaves), 14 (Stocktrek Images).

Cover photograph of Velociraptor (computer-generated
3D illustration) reproduced with permission of
Shutterstock (Michael Rosskothen).

Back cover photograph of Velociraptor reproduced with
permission of Shutterstock (Michael Rosskothen).

Every effort has been made to contact copyright holders
of material reproduced in this book. Any omissions will
be rectified in subsequent printings if notice is given to
the publisher.

6063 0109 12/15

Contents

Meet Velociraptor

Velociraptor was a dinosaur.

Dinosaurs lived long ago.

dinosaur

snake

crocodile

lizard

Dinosaurs were reptiles.
Snakes, crocodiles, and lizards
are reptiles that live today.

What Was Velociraptor Like?

Velociraptor was a small dinosaur.

Velociraptor was as big as a turkey!

feathers

Velociraptor may have had feathers.

tail

Velociraptor had a long tail.

Velociraptor ran on two legs.

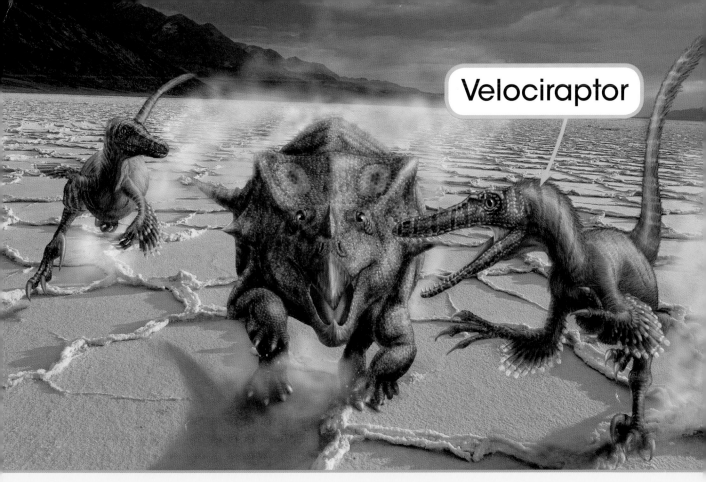

Velociraptor

Velociraptor was fast!

teeth

Velociraptor had sharp teeth.

claws

Velociraptor had long arms and sharp claws.

Velociraptor used its claws to attack other dinosaurs.

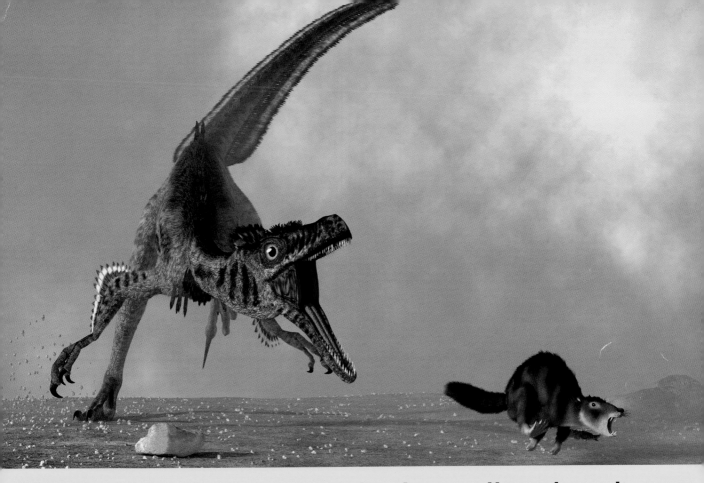

Velociraptor hunted small animals.

Where Is Velociraptor Now?

Velociraptor is extinct. There are no Velociraptors alive now.

All the dinosaurs died long ago.

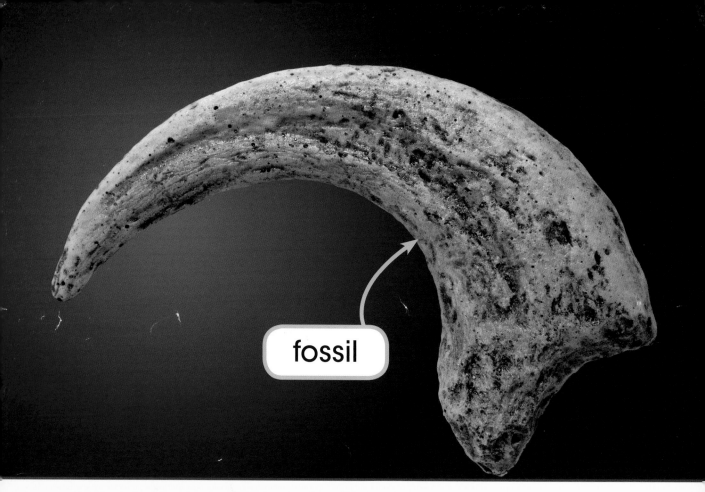

fossil

We learn about dinosaurs
from fossils.

Fossils are animal bones that
have turned to rock.

People find fossils in the ground.

Fossils show us what Velociraptor looked like.

Where In the World?

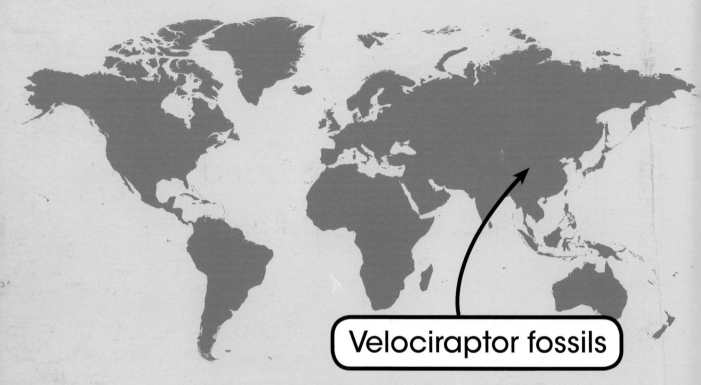

Velociraptor fossils

Velociraptor fossils have been found in Mongolia and China.

Picture Glossary

 **fossil** animal bones or parts of a plant that have turned into rock

 **reptile** cold-blooded animal. A lizard is a reptile.

How to Say It

Velociraptor: say
"veh-loss-ih-rap-tor"

Index

Notes for Parents and Teachers

Before Reading

Ask the children to name some dinosaurs. Ask them if dinosaurs are around today. Talk about how some dinosaurs ate plants and others ate other dinosaurs. Can they think of ways these dinosaurs might have been different? Have they heard of Velociraptor? Find out if they already know anything about this dinosaur.

After Reading

- Look at pictures of Velociraptor and compare them to pictures of birds. Can they see anything that looks the same? Talk about the size of Velociraptor, its feathers, and its claws. What are the differences between Velociraptor and birds? Talk about how scientists think birds are descended from dinosaurs.
- Make fossils. Roll out play dough and ask the children to cut out circles with cookie cutters. Then press small plastic toy dinosaurs sideways into the dough. Make a museum for your "fossils."